DESTINATION SPACE

NASA AND THE ASTRONAUTS

by Lisa J. Amstutz

FOCUS READERS

www.focusreaders.com

Focus Readers is distributed by North Star Editions:
sales@northstareditions.com | 888-417-0195

Produced for Focus Readers by Red Line Editorial.

Content Consultant: Dr. David A. Weintraub, Professor of Astronomy, Department of Physics & Astronomy, Vanderbilt University

Photographs ©: KSC/NASA, cover, 1; ITAR-TASS Photo Agency/Alamy, 4–5; HO/AP Images, 7; Marshall Space Flight Center Collection/NASA, 8; GRC/NASA, 10–11; Fine Art Images/Heritage Image Partnership Ltd/Alamy, 13; MSFC/NASA, 15, 16–17, 21; NASA, 19, 22–23; Harvey Georges/AP Images, 25; JSC/NASA, 26, 29, 30–31, 33, 35, 37, 38–39, 40, 42–43, 45

ISBN
978-1-63517-497-7 (hardcover)
978-1-63517-569-1 (paperback)
978-1-63517-713-8 (ebook pdf)
978-1-63517-641-4 (hosted ebook)

Library of Congress Control Number: 2017948057

Printed in the United States of America
Mankato, MN
November, 2017

ABOUT THE AUTHOR

Lisa J. Amstutz is the author of many children's books and articles. She specializes in topics related to science, nature, and agriculture. Her background includes a BA in biology and an MS in environmental science.

TABLE OF CONTENTS

CHAPTER 1

THE SPACE RACE BEGINS

On October 4, 1957, the Soviet Union launched a basketball-sized object into **orbit** around Earth. Known as *Sputnik 1*, this satellite was the first human-made object sent into space. News of the launch shocked people in the United States. At the time, the United States and the Soviet Union were racing to build the most nuclear weapons. Each country was eager to show its dominance.

Sputnik 1 **had several antennas that sent radio signals down to Earth.**

By the 1950s, the competition had turned toward space. It became known as the Space Race.

The United States had announced its plan to put a satellite into orbit in 1955. But the country's engineers had yet to succeed. With the launch of *Sputnik 1*, the United States was suddenly lagging behind. People feared that the Soviet Union might launch nuclear missiles next.

A month later, the Soviet Union launched a second satellite. *Sputnik 2* carried a dog named Laika. She was the first living being from Earth to orbit the planet. However, scientists had no way to bring her back to Earth, so she died in space.

The United States tried to launch a satellite in December 1957. But on the day of the launch, the rocket failed. It rose a few feet off the launchpad and exploded in a ball of fire. The satellite fell off the rocket and rolled away.

▲ The Soviet Union sent Laika to space aboard *Sputnik 2* on November 3, 1957.

The United States finally sent a satellite to space in January 1958. *Explorer 1* was launched aboard a Juno I rocket. It orbited Earth and collected data about Earth's atmosphere. The satellite measured cosmic rays and atmospheric temperatures. It also studied micrometeorites. These particles from space are small enough to enter Earth's atmosphere. This information helped scientists learn more about Earth's atmosphere and **magnetic field**.

➤ THE *EXPLORER I* SATELLITE

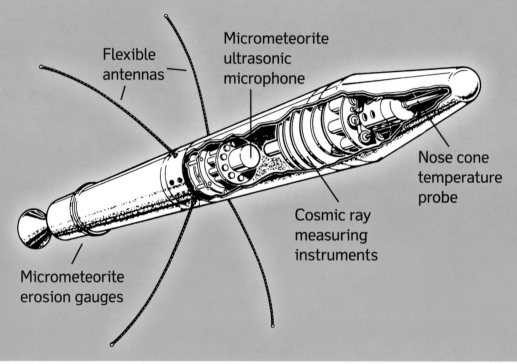

Flexible antennas

Micrometeorite ultrasonic microphone

Nose cone temperature probe

Cosmic ray measuring instruments

Micrometeorite erosion gauges

The next few launch attempts, including the *Explorer 2* satellite, were not successful. Finally, in March 1958, the *Vanguard 1* satellite successfully reached outer space. Later that month, *Explorer 3* also reached space. But the Soviet Union was not far behind. *Sputnik 3* launched two months later.

The US government did not want the Soviet Union to continue taking the lead in the Space Race. So, the US Congress created the National Aeronautics and Space Administration (NASA) in July 1958. This organization would coordinate the country's activity in space. This included both human and mechanical space exploration. Before NASA was created, the US military had directed these activities. But now NASA scientists and engineers would be in control. In 1958, NASA began working on Project Mercury. The project's goal was to launch a rocket carrying an astronaut into space.

THINK ABOUT IT ◀

Why would creating NASA help the United States be competitive in the Space Race?

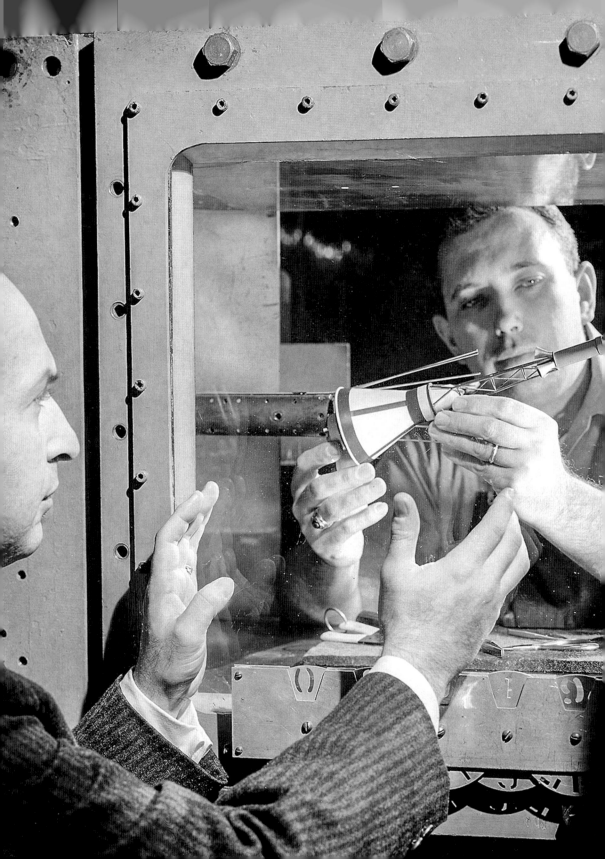

CHAPTER 2

TESTING SPACECRAFT

Sending an astronaut to space was an exciting goal, but it would be difficult. For one thing, the astronaut would be exposed to high levels of solar radiation. Also, temperatures in space can be as low as −455 degrees Fahrenheit (−270°C). Plus, there would be no air for the astronaut to breathe.

Surviving in space was not the only challenge. Returning safely to Earth would be difficult, too.

NASA scientists use a wind tunnel to test a model of the Mercury capsule in 1960.

The spacecraft would need to travel very quickly as it reentered Earth's atmosphere. This speed would create lots of **friction**, which would cause the spacecraft to get extremely hot.

A whole team of scientists went to work on these problems. They created a life-support system. This system would help astronauts survive the harsh conditions in space. Oxygen tanks supplied air for the astronauts to breathe. Space suits would protect astronauts from the cold of outer space. Helmets and visors also shielded astronauts from heat and radiation.

The Soviet Union was hard at work as well. Soviet scientists sent two dogs named Belka and Strelka into space in August 1960. This time, the rocket brought the dogs safely back to Earth. The Soviet Union was one step closer to sending a person to space.

▲ Belka (left) and Strelka shared their capsule with a rabbit, two rats, and 42 mice.

Meanwhile, NASA scientists and engineers tested many kinds of spacecraft and **propulsion** systems, including a rocket-powered airplane. Eventually, they decided to use a bell-shaped capsule for Project Mercury. Titanium coated the capsule's outside walls. The capsule also had a heat shield on its base. This shield would protect the capsule as it reentered Earth's atmosphere.

NASA sent up several unmanned test launches to make sure the Mercury capsule was safe. The first test used an Atlas rocket. But it caused an explosion. Therefore, NASA decided to use Mercury-Redstone rockets instead. The first Mercury-Redstone launch was in November 1960. But the engines shut off unexpectedly when the rocket was only inches above the ground. Engineers quickly worked to fix the problems with the engines. They successfully launched a Mercury-Redstone rocket in December.

Next, engineers were ready to test the capsule's life-support system. In January 1961, NASA sent a chimpanzee named Ham into space. Ham survived the flight, but there was a problem with the rocket's engines. This caused the spacecraft to fly higher and faster than expected. As a result, it landed more than 100 miles (161 km) from its

Ham wore a space suit during his flight in the Mercury capsule.

intended landing spot. NASA engineers wanted to fix this problem before sending a human into space, so they planned another test flight in March 1961.

CHAPTER 3

THE MERCURY ASTRONAUTS

As engineers perfected the Mercury capsule's design, NASA worked to select a group of astronauts. NASA was looking for experienced pilots who had some engineering expertise. In 1959, NASA began with 508 candidates. After several rounds of interviews and testing, NASA chose Scott Carpenter, Gordon Cooper, John Glenn, Virgil "Gus" Grissom, Walter Schirra, Alan Shepard, and Donald "Deke" Slayton.

The first astronauts were known as the Mercury Seven.

These seven men would be part of NASA's first missions to space.

The men trained for two years. They studied the Mercury capsule's systems and controls. The Mercury capsule had enough space for one astronaut. He lay on his back in the capsule's wider end. After the capsule was sealed, the astronaut could hardly move. But he could look out through a small window. He could also use the periscope above his head. This tube used mirrors and lenses to allow him to see objects outside his line of sight.

The astronauts also learned about the details of their missions. They practiced doing their mission tasks while wearing space suits. **Simulations** helped the astronauts prepare for the rapid **acceleration** and weightlessness they would experience during their flights to

THE MERCURY CAPSULE ◄

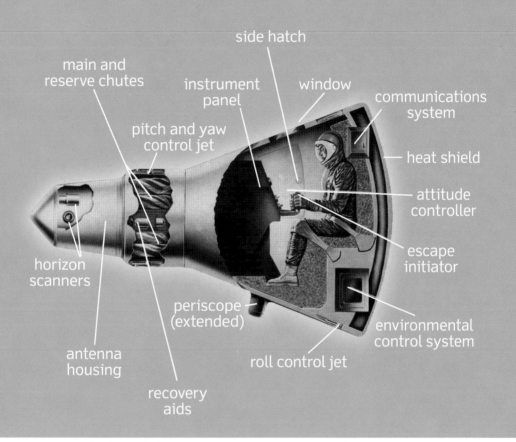

side hatch

main and reserve chutes

instrument panel

window

communications system

pitch and yaw control jet

heat shield

horizon scanners

attitude controller

escape initiator

periscope (extended)

antenna housing

environmental control system

roll control jet

recovery aids

space. The astronauts also used simulations to practice steering and controlling the spacecraft. In addition, the astronauts practiced opening the capsule's hatch and climbing out of the capsule.

This would prepare them to land in the ocean at the end of their mission.

However, before the first Project Mercury launch, the Soviet Union again took the lead. **Cosmonaut** Yuri Gagarin became the first person to enter space. On April 12, 1961, he orbited Earth one time. Soon after, Alan Shepard became the first American in space. Shepard did not fly high enough to go into orbit during his flight on May 5. But he did reach an altitude of 115 miles (185 km).

Once the capsule carrying Shepard reached its target altitude, the engine stopped. The rocket dropped away, and the capsule turned back toward Earth. A few minutes later, the capsule fired three retro-rockets to slow down. A parachute opened soon after to slow and steady the capsule's fall. Then the capsule landed in the

Man Enters Space

Close, t So Far,' ghs Cape

Had Hoped Own Launch

ANAVERAL, Fla. (AP) — The Redstone the United States had hoped would boost into space stands on a launching pad riet Union beat its firing date by at least

yet so far," commented a technician who om the Redstone to send one of America's astronauts on a short sub-orbital flight, hopefully late this month or early in May.

"If we hadn't had those trou-bles last fall and on the chimp shots this year, the

Soviet Officer Orbits Globe In 5-Ton Ship

Maximum Height Reached Reported As 188 Miles

MOSCOW (AP)—A Soviet astronaut has orbited the globe for more than an hour and returned safely to receive the plaudits of scientists and political leaders alike. Soviet announcement of the feat brought praise from President Kennedy and U. S. space experts left behind in the contest to put the first man into successful space flight.

By the Soviet account, Maj. Yuri Alekseyvich Gargarin, rode a five-ton spaceship once around the earth in an orbit taking an hour and 20 minutes. He was in the air a total of an hour and 48 minutes.

The whole sequence of events and the announcements relating to it raised a number of questions. The Soviet announcement said the flight

VON BRAUN'S REACTION:

To Keep Up

 Yuri Gagarin's flight made headlines around the world.

Atlantic Ocean, where it floated until a ship came to pick it up.

Shepard had spent 15 minutes in space. People around the world watched his mission on TV. Inspired by Shepard's success, President John F. Kennedy set a bold goal. On May 25, 1961, he called for the United States to land astronauts on the moon by the end of the decade.

CHAPTER 4

INTO ORBIT

President Kennedy's goal set off a flurry of activity at NASA. In July 1961, NASA launched a second **suborbital** mission. The *Liberty Bell 7* carried astronaut Gus Grissom into space. But the mission almost ended in tragedy. The *Liberty Bell 7* was the first capsule to use a new explosive hatch. At the end of the mission, the capsule landed in the ocean as planned. But as it bobbed in the water, the hatch blew off.

Gus Grissom (left) climbs into the *Liberty Bell 7*.

Water began rushing into the capsule. Grissom dived out and managed to stay afloat in the cold water until a helicopter arrived. But the *Liberty Bell 7* filled with water and sank.

Despite this setback, NASA was ready to send an astronaut into orbit. On February 20, 1962, John Glenn strapped himself into the seat of the *Friendship 7*. A powerful new Atlas rocket launched the capsule into space. Glenn completed three orbits during his flight, which lasted nearly five hours. Shepard and Grissom had only been in space for 15 minutes each. Doctors were concerned about what might happen to Glenn's body during his longer flight. They thought the movement of fluid in his ears could make him dizzy and sick. And they worried that his eyes would not be able to focus on the controls. Fortunately, neither of these things happened.

John Glenn trains inside the Mercury capsule.

But as Glenn orbited, an urgent problem arose. The spacecraft's heat shield seemed to be loose. If the heat shield fell off, the heat of reentering Earth's atmosphere would be fatal. The team of engineers and experts running the mission from the ground, known as mission control, created a plan. They told Glenn not to release the spacecraft's retro-rockets after firing them. The retro-rockets were strapped to the spacecraft.

△ Gordon Cooper trains during a simulated mission with the Mercury capsule.

They would be used to help slow the spacecraft down during reentry. Mission control hoped the retro-rockets would hold the heat shield in place. Parts of the retro-rockets burst into flames as the capsule reentered the atmosphere. But the capsule did not burn up, and Glenn landed safely. His flight made headlines around the world.

Glenn was the first American to orbit Earth. But others soon followed. Scott Carpenter orbited

Earth three times in May 1962. Later that year, Walter Schirra made six orbits around Earth. And in May 1963, Gordon Cooper completed the final Project Mercury mission. He orbited Earth 22 times during his 34-hour flight. These longer missions helped NASA prepare to send astronauts even farther into space.

NASA would also need to learn how to bring vehicles together in space. Several plans to reach the moon required using multiple spacecraft. Astronauts would need to dock, or connect, the spacecraft while in orbit. To do this, the astronauts would have to bring the spacecraft close together without crashing.

In 1962, two Soviet spacecraft reached orbit at the same time. The spacecraft stayed a few miles apart. But the Soviet Union had still come one step closer to joining two vehicles together.

JOHN GLENN

John Glenn was born on July 18, 1921. He grew up in Ohio. Glenn loved science, especially topics related to airplanes. After studying engineering in college, Glenn joined the Marines. He trained to fly fighter jets. Glenn was a fighter pilot during World War II (1939–1945) and the Korean War (1950–1953). After the Korean War, Glenn became a test pilot at the Naval Air Test Center. He flew many kinds of aircraft. In 1957, he set a record by flying from Los Angeles, California, to New York, New York, in only 3 hours and 23 minutes.

Glenn became an astronaut in 1959. He made his famous flight aboard the *Friendship 7* in 1962 as part of Project Mercury. Glenn continued to work at NASA until 1964. After that, he became a business executive. And from 1974 to 1999, he served as a US senator.

John Glenn's flight in the *Friendship 7* lasted 4 hours, 55 minutes, and 23 seconds.

In 1998, Glenn made history again as the oldest person to go to space. He traveled on the space shuttle *Discovery* when he was 77 years old. Glenn spent nine days aboard the shuttle. The crew orbited Earth 134 times during this mission. They also did experiments and **deployed** a spacecraft that would study the sun. Glenn continued to support space exploration for the rest of his life. He died in 2016 at the age of 95.

CHAPTER 5

PROJECT GEMINI BEGINS

In December 1961, NASA began a new program called Project Gemini. It was designed to identify and test the skills needed to send humans to the moon. Unlike the Mercury capsule, the Gemini capsule could hold two people. NASA hoped to use this larger capsule for longer missions. A powerful Titan II rocket would launch the capsule into space. Scientists would monitor how longer flights affected the human body.

The Gemini spacecraft and Titan II rocket stood 108 feet (33 m) tall when combined for launch.

NASA selected groups of new astronauts in 1962 and 1963. Thirteen of the astronauts, along with three of the Project Mercury astronauts, were chosen to be part of Project Gemini.

But before the first launch, the Soviet Union achieved another goal. In March 1965, cosmonaut Alexei Leonov became the first person to perform a **space walk**. Only days later, Gus Grissom and John Young rocketed to space for the Gemini 3 mission. They orbited Earth three times.

In June 1965, Edward White became the first American to perform a space walk. After the Gemini 4 capsule began orbiting Earth, White opened the capsule's hatch and stepped out into space. During his space walk, White wore a pressurized space suit. He also used a tether. This long cord connected him to the capsule. Inside the tether were an oxygen hose and a

⬙ In his right hand, Edward White holds the gas gun that allowed him to move.

communications system. White carried a small gun that blew puffs of gas. He used this gun to control his movements in space. After only three minutes, the gun ran out of gas. So, White pulled on the tether to move around the spacecraft.

White spent 23 minutes in space. Then he used the tether to pull himself back into the capsule.

The Gemini 5 mission tested how longer spaceflights affected astronauts. Next, NASA attempted to have two spacecraft meet up while orbiting Earth. The Gemini 6A spacecraft was supposed to launch in October 1965. NASA planned for it to meet up with the unmanned Agena target vehicle. But the Agena failed to go into orbit. So, NASA made a new plan. They would send two Gemini spacecraft into orbit instead.

The Gemini 7 spacecraft carried Frank Borman and Jim Lovell into space on December 4, 1965. They conducted experiments for a few days. On December 15, the Gemini 6A spacecraft launched with Walter Schirra and Thomas Stafford aboard. The two crews worked together to move the spacecraft into different formations.

▲ An artist's illustration of the Gemini 6A and Gemini 7
spacecraft in orbit together

The spacecraft came within 9 feet (2.7 m) of
each other. They stayed that close for more than
five hours. This important success showed that
spacecraft could fly near one another without
crashing. And it was the first spaceflight goal the
United States reached before the Soviet Union.
Now NASA was ready to try docking two vehicles.

THE GEMINI CAPSULE

The cone-shaped Gemini capsule was 18.6 feet (5.7 m) tall. Two astronauts sat side by side inside the capsule. They were surrounded by an instrument panel and controls. A hatch above each chair allowed the astronauts to leave the capsule for space walks.

At the bottom of the capsule, the retro-rocket section held eight rocket thrusters. These engines adjusted the capsule's direction as it flew through space. Below them, an equipment section held the supplies the astronauts would need during their mission. It carried drinking water, oxygen, a coolant pump, and fuel tanks. The electrical and communications systems were in the equipment section, too.

The Gemini capsule launched atop a Titan II rocket. The rocket had two sections, or stages. When the first stage used up its fuel, it dropped

▲ The Gemini capsule's circular base was 10 feet (3.0 m) wide.

off the capsule and fell into the ocean. Once the spacecraft began orbiting Earth, the second stage dropped off as well.

The rest of the Gemini spacecraft stayed together during the mission. Before the capsule reentered Earth's atmosphere, the equipment section fell off. Heat from friction caused it to burn up as it fell. The retro-rocket section turned the capsule. Then it fell off and burned up, too, exposing the capsule's heat shields. Only the capsule returned to Earth.

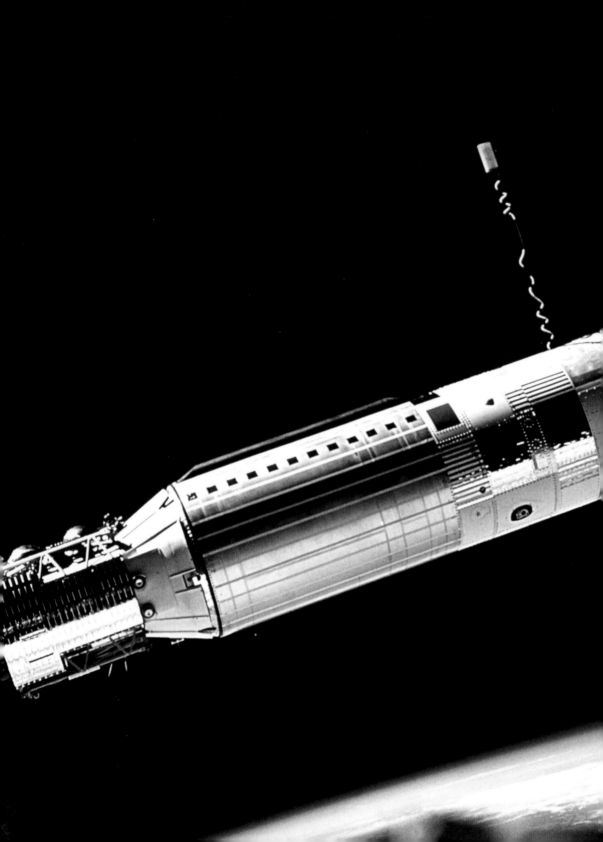

CHAPTER 6

FACING NEW CHALLENGES

Gemini 8 was NASA's first attempt to dock with the Agena. Pilot Neil Armstrong docked successfully. But both spacecraft began spinning rapidly. Armstrong disconnected from the Agena and pulled away, but the spinning continued. On the verge of blacking out, he shut down the main thrusters and fired backup thrusters. This stopped the spinning but used up most of the spacecraft's fuel. The rest of the mission had to be **aborted**.

This photo of the Agena target vehicle was taken from the Gemini 8 spacecraft.

▲ The US Navy picked up the Gemini 8 spacecraft and crew three hours after their emergency landing.

The astronauts made an emergency landing in the Pacific Ocean.

During Gemini 9A, Eugene Cernan performed a space walk to test the new Astronaut Maneuvering Unit (AMU). The AMU attached to the outside of the capsule. It looked like a huge backpack. Astronauts could disconnect from the tether and use the AMU's thrusters to move around. However, Cernan struggled to strap himself into the AMU. He got so hot that his visor fogged up, and he had to return to the capsule.

The next two missions also had problems. The Gemini 10 crew used more than twice as much fuel as planned while docking with the Agena. The Gemini 11 spacecraft docked well, but hard work during a space walk caused Richard Gordon to sweat inside his suit. This made it hard for him to see, so he had to end his space walk earlier than planned. NASA engineers worked to solve these issues before the final Gemini 12 mission.

THINK ABOUT IT ◁

Why might astronauts overheat during space walks?

CHAPTER 7

SHOOTING FOR THE MOON

Gemini 12 used several new pieces of technology. Despite a few minor problems, its crew successfully docked with the Agena. Handrails and frequent rest breaks helped Edwin "Buzz" Aldrin complete his space walk without overheating. When the crew landed in November 1966, Project Gemini was officially over.

NASA faced and overcame many challenges during Project Mercury and Project Gemini.

Scott Carpenter uses a simulator to train for a mission during Project Mercury.

These early missions taught scientists and engineers important lessons about space travel. During Project Mercury, NASA successfully put a spacecraft in orbit and developed ways to keep astronauts safe in space. Project Gemini helped NASA engineers perfect their strategies for launching and landing spacecraft. In addition, they learned how spacecraft could meet up and dock while orbiting Earth. The Gemini missions also tested astronauts' ability to stay in space for up to two weeks. Astronauts had even performed activities outside their spacecraft.

Landing on the moon still presented many new challenges. To reach the moon, a spacecraft would need to leave Earth's orbit. Then it would have to start orbiting the moon. Next, scientists would have to figure out how to send a spacecraft down to the moon's surface. Plus, the spacecraft would

▲ Mission control monitors the Gemini 7 flight.

need to carry enough food, oxygen, fuel, and other supplies for the journey. It would also need equipment to explore the moon's surface.

NASA would work on solving these problems during the Apollo program. And thanks to the many accomplishments of Project Mercury and Project Gemini, they were up for the challenge.

FOCUS ON
NASA AND THE ASTRONAUTS

Write your answers on a separate piece of paper.

1. How did Project Gemini help NASA prepare to send astronauts to the moon?

2. How do you think the astronauts felt when their spacecraft launched? Why?

3. Who was the first American to orbit Earth?

    A. Tom Stafford
    B. Walter Schirra
    C. John Glenn

4. Why did scientists use a powerful Titan II rocket to launch the Gemini capsule?

    A. The Gemini capsule was smaller and lighter, so it required less force to launch.
    B. The Gemini capsule was larger and heavier, so it required more force to launch.
    C. The Gemini capsule would not travel as far, so it required more force to launch.

Answer key on page 48.

GLOSSARY

aborted
Stopped a mission or flight earlier than originally planned.

acceleration
A change in motion, such as speeding up or slowing down.

cosmonaut
An astronaut from the Soviet Union or Russia.

deployed
Carried something into orbit and then released it into space.

friction
A force generated by the rubbing of one thing against another.

magnetic field
The space around an object (such as a moon or planet) in which its magnetic force can be detected.

orbit
To repeatedly follow a curved path around another object because of gravity.

propulsion
The force that moves a vehicle forward.

simulations
Things that are made to look or feel like something else, often for training.

space walk
When an astronaut goes outside a spacecraft and moves around in space.

suborbital
Below the height or speed required to send a vehicle into orbit.

TO LEARN MORE

BOOKS

Kelley, K. C. *Astronauts!* Broomall, PA: Mason Crest, 2015.

Nagelhout, Ryan. *Astronauts*. New York: PowerKids Press, 2016.

Reichl, Eugen. *Project Mercury*. Atglen, PA: Schiffer Publishing, 2016.

NOTE TO EDUCATORS

Visit **www.focusreaders.com** to find lesson plans, activities, links, and other resources related to this title.

INDEX

Answer Key: 1. Answers will vary; **2.** Answers will vary; **3.** C; **4.** B